WOMEN WHO FINISH

40 DAY DEVOTIONAL TO SET YOUR LIFE ON PURPOSE, PERMANENTLY.

ROBYN-ANN YOUNG

Because **finishing** is a mindset before it's a method.

Let's change our mind.

Copyright © 2016 by Robyn-Ann Young. All rights reserved.

You are permitted to print a copy of this document for your personal use. Outside of that, no part of this publication may be reproduced, stored, or transmitted in any form or by any means electronic, mechanical, photocopying, recording, scanning, or otherwise, except as permitted under Section 107 or 108 of the 1976 United States Copyright Act, without the prior written permission of the author. Requests to the author and publisher for permission should be address to the following email: hi@robyn-ann.com

Limitation of liability/disclaimer of warranty: While the publisher and author have used their best efforts in preparing this guide workbook, they make no representations or warranties with respect to the accuracy or completeness of the contents of this document and specifically disclaim any implied warranties of merchantability or fitness for particular purpose. No warranty may be created or extended by sales representatives, promoters, or written sales materials.

The advice and strategies contained herein may not be suitable for your situation. You should consult with a professional where appropriate. Neither the publisher nor author shall be liable for any loss of profit or any other commercial damages, including but not limited to special, incidental, consequential, or other damages.

HELLO GORGEOUS!

I am so excited that you decided to take this journey with me. Feasting and meditating on the word of God has been one of the major habits that helped me overcome a porn addiction and purposeless living. So I know you will come out on the other side of this devotional transformed also.

By the way, I'm Robyn-Ann, a writer and speaker that gets roaring to empower virtuous women to dominate their purpose, passions, and purity. I have a blast serving up eBooks, digital courses and coaching programs that move women to get clear and get going in God's dreams for their life.

Because, as I've figured out, answering His call is the quickest way to lasting peace, pleasure, and prosperity. So I'm hoping these affirmations remind you to prioritize the Good News that Jesus has deposited in you beloved. Let this devotional stir a fresh fire to take God seriously, and push into His promises without fear or apology.

We already know that faith without works is nothing but a rotting corpse. Therefore I've been praying for this devotional to breathe fresh commitment into those dreams God painted on your heart. You're a pretty big deal in His eyes and He's been waiting to get back to the adventure He saved you for. I'm serious!

I mean, no one goes out of their way to die for you unless they don't want to live without you. Right?! Exactly.

Let's kick procrastination and perfectionism to the curb and get back to the business of finishing in His presence and power. Because well done is better than well said. Let's roar!

p.s. feel free to give me a shout at any time, for any reason, via the websites or email below. Chat soon

Robyn-Ann.com | hi@robyn-ann.com | @robynannl on Instagram | #WomenWhoFinish

TABLE OF CONTENTS

IDENTITY
Agreeing with who you already are 1

IDENTITY DAY 1 | I AM SAVED 5

IDENTITY DAY 2 | I AM A BELIEVER 11

IDENTITY DAY 3 | I AM A LIONESS 17

IDENTITY DAY 4 | I AM A CITIZEN OF HEAVEN 23

IDENTITY DAY 5 | I AM BEAUTIFUL 29

FRIENDSHIP WITH GOD
Your highest privilege and purpose. **33**

FRIENDSHIP DAY 1 | I AM GOD'S FRIEND 37

FRIENDSHIP DAY 2 | I HEAR GOD'S VOICE 43

FRIENDSHIP DAY 3 | I GUARD GOD'S FRIENDSHIP 49

FRIENDSHIP DAY 4 | I HAVE THE BEST CONNECT 55

FRIENDSHIP DAY 5 | I AM IN THE INNER CIRCLE 61

DISCIPLINE
Giving up what you want now for what you want most. **65**

DISCIPLINE DAY 1 | I HAVE TODAY 69

DISCIPLINE DAY 2 | I DIRECT MY LIGHT 75

DISCIPLINE DAY 3 | I OBEY FAITH NOT FEELINGS 81

DISCIPLINE DAY 4 | I LEAD MY HEART 87

DISCIPLINE DAY 5 | I GET IT DONE 93

GODLY
PROVISION
Using what God gives to get to what God promised.
....**97**

PROVISION DAY 1 | I AM SATISFIED BY GOD 101

PROVISION DAY 2 | I AM PROVIDED FOR 107

PROVISION DAY 3 | I AM A GOOD INVESTMENT 113

PROVISION DAY 4 | I AM IN GOD'S HOUSE 119

PROVISION DAY 5 | I CAN ASK FOR WHATEVER I NEED 125

PURITY
Guarding God's vision so you can hear His voice. ..129

PURITY DAY 1 | I AM PART OF A FAMILY 133

PURITY DAY 2 | I LIVE IN THE LIGHT 139

PURITY DAY 3 | I HAVE AUTHORITY 145

PURITY DAY 4 | I SEE WHAT GOD SEES 151

PURITY DAY 5 | I AM GOD'S RESTING PLACE 157

COURAGE
Being confident about your Father's business. 161

COURAGE DAY 1 | I AM LOVED 165

COURAGE DAY 2 | I AM ALLERGIC TO ANXIETY 171

COURAGE DAY 3 | I FIGHT FOR MY INHERITANCE ...177

COURAGE DAY 4 | I AM THE LIGHT IN THE ROOM 183

COURAGE DAY 5 | I SERVE CHRIST ONLY 189

FOCUS
Making heaven's purpose your priority **193**

FOCUS DAY 1 | I PURSUE PURPOSE NOT PAPER 197

FOCUS DAY 2 | I DOMINATE MY DESIRES 203

FOCUS DAY 3 | I FEED MY SPIRIT MAN 209

FOCUS DAY 4 | I PLAY TO WIN 215

FOCUS DAY 5 | I MOVE WITH CLARITY & STRATEGY 221

PASSION
Pursuing God's call without apology **225**

PASSION DAY 1 | I AM FREE, PERIOD. 229

PASSION DAY 2 | I AM WIRED TO WIN 235

PASSION DAY 3 | I AM CHOSEN 241

PASSION DAY 4 | I RUN WITH THE VISION 247

PASSION DAY 5 | I FINISH WHAT I START 253

Pinpointing Purpose Questions **257**

IDENTITY

Agreeing with who you already are.

I AM SAVED

> "FOR AT ONE TIME YOU WERE DARKNESS, BUT NOW YOU ARE LIGHT IN THE LORD.
> WALK AS CHILDREN OF LIGHT."
>
> – Ephesians 5:8

IDENTITY DAY 1 | I AM SAVED

"For at one time you were darkness, but now you are light in the Lord. Walk as children of light."

– Ephesians 5:8

If you cannot verbalize what God has done for you personally, then it's possible that you're not able to recognize all that has been done. Even more, not knowing what you've been saved from should make you ask yourself "Am I truly saved?"

Because a saved person should be aware of the sin, guilt, and darkness that God rescued you from. If you're not sure, then it's time to take an honest look at whether you really see the Gospel as Good News, or just a good story. You're probably just calling yourself a Christian but still living the life you would've lived if Christ didn't die.

If you truly believe Jesus was crucified to pay the price for your sin and shame, then it's time to commit to walking out that freedom in every area of your life. Embrace your new identity as "daughter of the Most High God." Own the title of holiness that has been given to you in Christ Jesus, even when you don't feel like it.

And like the crown placed upon your head, you will begin to feel the weight to walk worthy of the gift someone else has purchased for you.

Don't settle for the ruin of sin, call on your King!

JOURNAL PROMPT

Write down 2-3 hopeless situations or struggles that were facing you before you encountered Jesus. What hope do you now have in God to replace those lies of defeat? Does your life reflect the distinct transfer from darkness to light spoken of in Colossians 1:13-14?

I AM A BELIEVER

"HOW LONG WILL YOU GO LIMPING BETWEEN TWO DIFFERENT OPINIONS? IF THE LORD IS GOD, FOLLOW HIM; BUT IF BAAL, THEN FOLLOW HIM."

–1 Kings 18:21

IDENTITY DAY 2 | I AM A BELIEVER

"How long will you go limping between two different opinions? If the Lord is God, follow him; but if Baal, then follow him."

-1 Kings 18:21

Your behavior is only a reflection of how you identify yourself. For example, if you constantly repeat how lazy or defeated you are, you keep giving yourself permission to procrastinate when you don't feel like doing something.

However, if you continually acknowledge the overcomer you are in Christ, you filter the lies of failure through this truth and start breaking agreements with that spirit of hopelessness. Such an atmosphere makes it much harder for bad habits or quitting to thrive. Plus, focusing on what's true motivates you to endure until you see that truth proven in every situation.

Accepting God as Lord of your life once and for all demands that you give Him Lordship over your identity also. You have to prioritize His Word regardless of what your brain or culture is shouting. Otherwise, you live a lukewarm life, always limping between 2 opinions – paralyzed between faith and fear.

Which leads to a waste of mental energy and willpower. Because zigzagging between worry and prayer will only keep you circling in the same dessert and circumstance year after year. And frankly, *ain't nobody got time for that.*

Decide once and for all that the straightest and quickest path to your purpose and pleasure is believing what God says about the situation. Because it is.

You are a believer, not a doubleminded woman. Selah.

JOURNAL PROMPT

Ask God to reveal any sin, habits or attitudes that are sourced from our culture or laziness and not from the Word of God. Decide to break your agreement with that belief, and to stand on what God says about you instead.

I AM A LIONESS

"BEHOLD, A PEOPLE! AS A LIONESS IT RISES UP AND AS A LION IT LIFTS ITSELF."

-Numbers 23:24a

IDENTITY DAY 3 | I AM A LIONESS

"Behold, a people! As a lioness it rises up and as a lion it lifts itself."

-Numbers 23:24a

This identification of the lioness was God's exclamation over His people Israel as they moved through the wilderness. Mind you, these are the same people that call themselves grasshoppers when God instructs them to take a hold of the land He promised.

Why do we do talk back to God about who we are? As if He doesn't clearly see our humanness which He created. Yet, the glory that we are perfectly fashioned to carry is in Him.

NEVER FORGET: *We were made frail and hollow to be the perfect dwelling place for His Spirit and power.*

Your God is a roaring lion of the tribe of Judah and has called you to walk alongside Him in purpose and authority. Therefore, that makes you a lioness with a kingdom to reign over.

Get bold about knowing the promises that you've been crowned with. And decide to stop talking back to the Holy Spirit and what He says about you.

That way, you can seriously put your hand to everything that is commissioned by God, to rule in love and power. You have no need to fear sheep who have not been sent by God. So stand firm against every resistance that comes, and see it as opposition to God Himself when you are in His will. And we know that anyone who opposes God is destined to fall – doesn't matter if it's a sword or a stone. Which means we can David any Goliath that comes our way this season.

Because the woman who fears God has nothing else to fear.

JOURNAL PROMPT

Write out five promises from God's Word that you can boldly confess about yourself daily. Get sticky notes or index cards and post these confessions around your room, car, office, etc. as a reminder of what is true.

I AM A CITIZEN OF HEAVEN

"FEAR NOT, LITTLE FLOCK, FOR IT IS YOUR FATHER'S GOOD PLEASURE TO GIVE YOU THE KINGDOM."

–Luke 12:32

IDENTITY DAY 4 | I AM A CITIZEN OF HEAVEN

"Fear not, little flock, for it is your Father's good pleasure to give you the kingdom."

–Luke 12:32

As Christians, it's so easy to become known for what we don't accomplish, rather than what we do accomplish.

This leads to a deprived spiritual man that's been kept hostage, unable to venture out into the unknown fields of faith and missional adventure for fear of what the flesh he's wrapped in might do.

But this is not the life Jesus died for us to live.

His last words to his saints were *"GO...."* (Matthew 28:19), not *"DON'T GO or you will stumble and surely fall"*. He declared that all authority in heaven and earth had been given to him so we were now free to venture into the world's hopelessness bearing His light, legacy, and leadership.

Yes, it would be unwise to live a defenseless life without core disciplines such as community, accountability, prayer and fasting. But these are just the beginnings of a winning strategy, or the Christian call to be salt of the earth. Equipped with the breastplate of righteousness, helmet of salvation, the belt of truth, and more – we have now been left in the earth to advance on the enemy and usher in heaven to earth with our prayers and lifestyle examples.

What would you do if you knew you had all of heaven backing you?

Then it's time to do it, because you are already a kingdom citizen, seated in high places – but just wrapped in flesh to infiltrate earth with heavenly solutions, beauty, and ideas. So go.

Become known for what you were brave enough to do.

JOURNAL PROMPT

Is there anything that you have been fearful to do? Decide to ignore fear and ask the Father to grace you with the wisdom on how to walk it out this season. Set a deadline in your journal and pray for an accountability partner to keep you brave and obedient.

I AM BEAUTIFUL

"AND OUT OF THE GROUND THE LORD GOD MADE TO SPRING UP EVERY TREE THAT IS PLEASANT TO THE SIGHT AND GOOD FOR FOOD."

–Genesis 2:9

IDENTITY DAY 5 | I AM BEAUTIFUL

"And out of the ground the Lord God made to spring up every tree that is pleasant to the sight and good for food."

–Genesis 2:9

You were made beautiful, with more value than each tree which God calls pleasant.

He gives both external and internal beauty. Both are to be stewarded, because one without the other can dull our effectiveness as ambassadors of heaven. A beautiful fruit on the outside with worms on the inside is a turn-off. The same can be said for a gorgeous woman with a graceless heart. Similarly, a lack-luster fruit on the outside can be overlooked even if its insides are tasty. So we do not have to choose one or the other.

Let's feel free to be a Sarah, a Rachel, or an Esther - who were all beautiful for men to behold and fruitful in the way they served their culture, their husbands and God. God created and rejoices in both outward beauty and inward fruitfulness. We are designed to showcase the attributes God has given us, not by trying to be a fruit that we're not. By realizing, instead, that the traits and skills Holy Spirit wired into us personally is going to be an awesome blessing to someone's life. But we will only see it play out beautifully when we actually celebrate this God-given identity.

Because beauty is in the eye of the Creator.

Also, let's be mindful that if we draw attention to our tree by its beauty, we should have substance ready to offer those who come near. Jesus demonstrates his disgust for fruit*less*ness towards the fig tree in Matthew 21:18-19, so let's not draw men to our tree in vain.

JOURNAL PROMPT

Ask God to lead you to someone that you can be of service to today. It doesn't have to be extravagant; simply be willing to plant a fruitful seed. Don't forget to package it with a beautiful smile :)

FRIENDSHIP WITH GOD

Your highest privilege and purpose.

I AM GOD'S FRIEND

"NO LONGER DO I CALL YOU SERVANTS, FOR THE SERVANT DOES NOT KNOW WHAT HIS MASTER IS DOING; BUT I HAVE CALLED YOU FRIENDS."

–John 15:15a

FRIENDSHIP DAY 1 | I AM GOD'S FRIEND

"No longer do I call you servants, for the servant does not know what his master is doing; but I have called you friends."

–John 15:15a

What did God have in mind when He created you? Don't get to the end of your life never having asked that question. It would be a waste of your existence if you left this earth letting everyone use you but God.

You *literally* DO NOT have time for that because your time on earth was specifically given to you for His purposes. , Moreover God didn't create you to be His robotic task machine, but He made you in His image so the vision could be mutually shared in friendship.

You have been wired to understand God's heart. As friends, there is an ability to share your desires with God and have Him take it seriously, and vice versa. Jesus reveals His passion to destroy the works of darkness, set captives free, and preach Good News because just like us, He loves to share the experience with like-minded souls.

Exciting, right?!

Let's schedule some quality prayer time this week to maximize friendship with Our Father, and unite our heart to His in love.

JOURNAL PROMPT

Share the vulnerable desires of your heart and ask God to share His as you linger to listen in silence. Read Isaiah 61:1-3 if you need help hearing the things that get God excited. Then allow the admiration of each other's passions to stir a flame that compels you to move in love, instead of duty.

I HEAR GOD'S VOICE

> "THUS THE LORD USED TO SPEAK TO MOSES FACE TO FACE, AS A MAN SPEAKS TO HIS FRIEND."

–Exodus 33:11a

FRIENDSHIP DAY 2 | I HEAR GOD'S VOICE

"Thus the Lord used to speak to Moses face to face, as a man speaks to his friend."

–Exodus 33:11a

I doubt a modern-day Moses would be aching over whether to catch '50 Shades of Grey' on Netflix or call his girlfriend over at midnight.

Not because he is a boring human or hated fun – but he enjoys such a rich privilege and adventure with God, his heart lacks nothing. His joy is so full and his responsibility so awesome, that every free moment finds him drawing near to God to gain greater perspective and insight on his life.

Not only for his life, but he is able to get a vision for God's people around him. He has developed a passion for seeing them walk into their full provision as those "chosen by God".

And we have been called into that same privilege as Moses – nothing less. If we know God, we know His voice, because we share the same Spirit. So just pause at any moment to tune in and ask for His direction. Then pay attention – it won't usually be an audible voice. Instead, watch out for a fresh visual, thought, emotion, or knowing that lines up with God's voice and gives you the peace to proceed.

"My sheep hear my voice, and I know them, and they follow me." –John 10:27

Let's not settle for good Christian morals when we can have great instead. We have the very presence of God daily with us to proclaim His power, and to stand out enough to shift our culture.

"For how shall it be known that I have found favor in your sight, I and your people? Is it not in your going with us, so that we are distinct, I and your people, from every other people on the face of the earth?" –Exodus 33:16.

JOURNAL PROMPT

Thank God for the imagination and ability to hear His voice. Practice hearing His voice by sitting in silence, and then writing down anything true, pure, praiseworthy or excellent that pops into your mind or imagination. Now ask Him to commune with you today and be ready throughout the day to write jot down what He speaks.

I GUARD GOD'S FRIENDSHIP

"THE FRIENDSHIP OF THE LORD IS FOR THOSE WHO FEAR HIM, AND HE MAKES KNOWN TO THEM HIS COVENANT."

–Psalm 25:14

FRIENDSHIP DAY 3 | I GUARD GOD'S FRIENDSHIP

"The friendship of the Lord is for those who fear him, and he makes known to them his covenant."

–Psalm 25:14

I pity the fool who takes for granted God's invitation to friendship. My culture would call me foolish for choosing to abstain from casual sex or getting cable TV. Yet, the same audience offers admiration when a great artist refrains from these same activities to preserve his focus on producing great artwork. Why? Because perspective is everything.

I believe the Christian's choice to abstain from "casual pleasures" is seen as folly because our lives don't produce any joyful fruit or greater outcome as a result. Instead, our abstinence often catches us in idle boredom, drooling over worldly creations. Or desperately trying to get our culture's attention by showing them our counterfeit versions of what they already produced. Let's stop this mad pursuit of being relevant.

Diving into our "access granted" freedom to be intimate with Christ and the Holy Spirit will empower us to be relevant to society's questions and issues, without us even trying. But until we are able to **identify the missing pleasures of God in our own lives** which keep making sin attractive – we will have no peace to offer anyone else.

As John Piper often reminds us, "God is most glorified in us when we are most satisfied in Him."

Let's enjoy our God.

JOURNAL PROMPT

Ask the Lord to reveal to you any areas in your life that are disconnected from His pleasures. Get honest and don't be afraid to admit places where you are unhappy, or duties that you find it hard to be joyful in. Then ask the Lord for His perspective, and how you can infuse His intended pleasure for that activity – so you don't leave it void for sin that lure you away in it.

I HAVE THE BEST CONNECT

"As I was in my prime, when the friendship of God was upon my tent."

–Job 29:4

FRIENDSHIP DAY 4 | I HAVE THE BEST CONNECT

"As I was in my prime, when the friendship of God was upon my tent."

–Job 29:4

It's all about who you know, and you know the Greatest One of all time. Literally. The friendship of God will always lead to the prime version of ourselves. That's why it hurts to see believers more saddened over missing out on an episode of Empire, than on missing out on their own heavenly empire.

We're not missing out on the world – the world is missing out on the real us!

Sacrificing intimate friendship with God to remain relevant to worldly events leaves you with no power to do anything about what you know is happening in your culture. Forget what you heard, you do have to be heavenly minded to truly be of any earthly good. It's time to change our minds, aka repent.

Let me encourage you daughter, the King knows the best you. This is why He is beckoning you closer to perfume you in the glory that you're seeking in everything else. Only His version of you wins.

Draw near to your Father, so He can train you in the way of royals and give you the fresh perspective that will bring peace and strategy for this season of your life. His friendship will effortlessly reveal how to win friends and influence people.

JOURNAL PROMPT

Plan a date with God and write down some overdue tasks that your spirit man has been craving (ie. books to read, songs to write, etc). Set aside a *specific slot* on your calendar where you can spend some uninterrupted time in His presence and His Word. He welcomes and enjoys your company.

I AM IN THE INNER CIRCLE

"BUT KNOW THAT THE LORD HAS SET APART THE GODLY FOR HIMSELF;
THE LORD HEARS WHEN I CALL TO HIM."

–Psalm 4:3

FRIENDSHIP DAY 5 | I AM IN THE INNER CIRCLE

**"But know that the Lord has set apart
the godly for himself;
the Lord hears when I call to him."**

–Psalm 4:3

You have been saved for a Person, and for a purpose. We must get to know who we've been saved for, or we'll only return to the same failing things we've been saved from. Same with the "what" – if we don't understand the new kingdom lifestyle we now get to enjoy, we'll return to the lifestyle of darkness. And that would be a waste of blood being spilled on your behalf.

We will waste what we don't understand or know exists.

The Master of the Universe has called you out of confusion to have all-access conversations with you. Let that reality sit and process. Is that really something you want to pass up each day?

If God saved us to share in His heart and mission, then let's focus on asking Him which gifts and agendas we need to prioritize each day.

This will also help us understand why the enemy has been trying to block our shots, and to stop taking it personal. Actually, do take it personal and vow to not be deceived by the losing team. God allows us to encounter opposition because it sharpens us and teaches us to run with more focus. We cannot afford to run aimlessly like someone with no heritage.

Our King is on the move, let's keep in step.

JOURNAL PROMPT

Make a list of all the things you need to accomplish today. Now ask the Holy Spirit for the wisdom on how to prioritize what's important vs what just feels urgent. Identify the top 3 things that would give us peace and move us forward in our purpose if nothing else got done. Now focus on those 3 things and go! (Achieving anything else is bonus).

DISCIPLINE

Giving up what you want now for what you want most.

I HAVE TODAY

> "BEHOLD, NOW IS THE FAVORABLE TIME; BEHOLD, NOW IS THE DAY OF SALVATION."
>
> –2 Corinthians 6:2b

DISCIPLINE DAY 1 | I HAVE TODAY

"Behold, now is the favorable time; behold, now is the day of salvation."

–2 Corinthians 6:2b

Living in the past and waiting on the future allows for no advancements in the present. Many of us wish we could change our testimonies or just jump to the future to really start living. However, we are intentionally created to affect change in the present only.

The "now" is all God gave us, because it's enough.

Even more than being enough, it's necessary.

We have to stop treating the present as some blah existence to survive until our fantasies come true. Instead, let's realize that present moments are the bricks we use to lay the foundation for that amazing future. If we can't practice the discipline, joy, and gratitude needed to control our attitudes now, then we will not make the correct choices that produce tomorrow's contrasting results.

It will always be "today", and that is good news. So whatever misery you are waiting on to be "saved" from, ask God to show you that He is that joy for you <u>today</u>.

Salvation is not just a one-day thing, it is every day's hope now that we have Jesus. Don't waste it by waiting for someday. On earth as it is in heaven begins today, just ask.

JOURNAL PROMPT

Make a list of all the things that are not "going right" in your life. Underneath each problem, ask the Father to give you His solution and His perspective. How does His perspective differ from yours? Thank God for the grace to see His perspective in every situation, even as we wait for His solutions.

I DIRECT MY LIGHT

"YOU ARE THE LIGHT OF THE WORLD. A CITY SET ON A HILL THAT CANNOT BE HIDDEN."

–Matthew 5:14

DISCIPLINE DAY 2 | I DIRECT MY LIGHT

"You are the light of the world. A city set on a hill that cannot be hidden."

–Matthew 5:14

Lioness, the beauty and compassion God has given you naturally shines without you even trying. Don't downplay it or defer it to someone else. Put it on a platform!

Settling for good while serving a great God is contradictory.

The Holy Spirit was not given to you for mediocre living. Whatever ideas and skills God has been revealing to you are for His service to the world. They are not yours to sit on. The light in you refuses to be hidden – and neglecting your DNA to shine will eventually have you seeking out inappropriate ways to get attention. (Stop picking up that boy's calls!).

No matter who you are, you're going to pursue value and pleasure in something.

Discipline, however, is you choosing to direct your energy to healthy pursuits instead of regretful ones. Without discipline, you'll end up reacting to whatever wind blows your way each day, instead of making small steps to train and unleash your own fire.

Let's take stock of the dreams and desires God has put on our hearts to cultivate. What message of freedom has He lit in your heart that you would be selfish to keep from others? It's time to carve out time and opportunity to showcase them so others can see and glorify your Heavenly Dad.

JOURNAL PROMPT

Review those desires the Lord has placed inside of you and jot them down. Ask Him to give you the wisdom on how you can put your skills to use to advance His Kingdom this week. Remember, He didn't give you these gifts to keep to yourself.

I OBEY FAITH NOT FEELINGS

"IF ANYONE WOULD COME AFTER ME, LET HIM DENY HIMSELF AND TAKE UP HIS CROSS AND FOLLOW ME."

–Matthew 16:24

DISCIPLINE DAY 3 | I OBEY FAITH NOT FEELINGS

"If anyone would come after me, let him deny himself and take up his cross and follow me."

–Matthew 16:24

Many are called, yet few are chosen. The call to salvation goes out to many, yet only the repentant are chosen to be His disciples. If we have been called His, let's bear fruit in keeping with repentance (Matthew 3:8). God is expecting fruitfulness (read productive activity and godly results) even at a young age. And if you are in Him, He will cut off any branch in you that's not bearing fruit.

This week, choose to recognize and rejoice in His call to discipline various areas of life. Allowing Him to prune you reveals that you truly are His and delight in His leadership.

God will not work on your behalf while your devotion is set on our idols. He is a jealous and holy God, not a prostitute. **We cannot just pimp Him for our needs.**

Let's regard Him as holy in our choices and say yes to his instructions to "throw off every weight that hinders" (Hebrews 12:1). Listennnn, God knows what He is talking about and always wins because He moves with wisdom. This is why He calls us to be wise also.

Being wise means planning for the long journey ahead by following the guidance of The Only Person who knows where the path ends. Don't be like the foolish virgins who only thought their self-righteousness thus far would get them into the kingdom, so they didn't keep their oil fresh by tuning into God's commands to stay ready. (Matthew 25:1-13).

You are not smarter than God.

JOURNAL PROMPT

Ask God to reveal any lukewarm or disobedient areas in your life blocking true intimacy with Him. Now thank Him for the grace to close those doors and not reopen them. Focus on the doors (promises) you know He is about to open instead, and fill up on the Word so you don't get tempted to go off on your own wisdom when you feel empty.

I LEAD MY HEART

"OUT OF THE HEART FLOWS THE ISSUES OF LIFE."

–Proverbs 4:23b

DISCIPLINE DAY 4 | I LEAD MY HEART

"Out of the heart flows the issues of life."

–Proverbs 4:23b

Contrary to popular belief, following your heart (like media loves to shout) will only result in confusion and security.

Don't follow your heart, lead it.

Because quite frankly, your heart will sometimes be wrong. Your heart only reproduces whatever you've been feeding it. So if that diet has not been 100% truth, then it cannot lead you based on 100% truth.

That's why living by our culture's mantra to "do what feels right" will only produce an unstable life at best, or a dark life at worst. You will have no one to blame, because your heart was simply spitting out a mashup of the random experiences you've had along the way. Furthermore, such a lifestyle has no reference point to identify when you're going off course.

Lead your heart with the Word of God which will remain true - no matter what lies culture or you emotions want to tell you that day.

Only God knows the end of the story and can show you how to arrive at your destiny's truest desire. His love will never lead you astray, and comes with a faithful guide to differentiate which truths are absolute enough to stand on and which thoughts are only sinking sand.

"Therefore, since we are receiving a kingdom that cannot be shaken, let us be thankful, and so worship God acceptably with reverence and awe." (Hebrews 12:28)

JOURNAL PROMPT

Be conscious of what you are feeding your spirit man today. Pray for revelation on any emotions that you've been living from or reacting to as truth. Be intentional about guarding your heart from words, visuals, music, or places that would cause your heart to be distracted from God's crazy amazing Good News.

I GET IT DONE

> "TO OBEY IS BETTER THAN SACRIFICE, AND TO LISTEN THAN THE FAT OF RAMS."

–1 Samuel 15:22b

DISCIPLINE DAY 5 | I GET IT DONE

"To obey is better than sacrifice, and to listen than the fat of rams."

–1 Samuel 15:22b

Practice makes perfect, not humans. Many of us to get obsessed waiting on the right conditions before moving on what God spoke. For others, waiting is the hard part and you're always striving to improve the situation until God decides to move.

Both attitudes often produce rebellion to God's directions and can be traced to a root of pride or people-pleasing. Today's theme verse is actually part of a rebuke to King Saul who had a constant reputation for prioritizing what the people wanted - especially when God's instructions seemed too extreme or impractical in the moment.

As someone recovering from a "messiah complex", I've learned that it's best to let situations fall apart if God has asked me to step back and let Him work. It may be hard to watch, but you'll realize that He is much better at mending brokenness than you are at holding things together.

So if God speaks on any area in your life, just execute it without looking at your circumstance. **Focus on getting it done, rather than getting it perfect before men.** Even if "getting it done" just means waiting.

For as Paul points out, "if I were still trying to please man, I would not be a servant of Christ" (Galatians 1:10).

JOURNAL PROMPT

Write down every desire you have before the Lord. Ask Him for the discernment on which dreams need to be executed now in your imperfect strength and which ones need to be submitted to His glorious timing. Meditate on Psalm 37:4 as a reminder to delight in Him as you trust Him to bring every desire to pass.

GODLY PROVISION

Using what God gives to get to what God promised.

I AM SATISFIED BY GOD

"THE RIGHTEOUS HAS ENOUGH TO SATISFY HIS APPETITE."

–Proverbs 13:25a

PROVISION DAY 1 | I AM SATISFIED BY GOD

"The righteous has enough to satisfy his appetite."

–Proverbs 13:25a

It's so easy for us to leave church on Sunday rejoicing in God's goodness and then show up to work on Monday complaining about what we are lacking. Lord, we repent for our double-mindedness.

Is God really enough, or not?

If He is, we have to do better at filtering the words that we speak in unfavorable situations. God watches over His word to perform it – but if we are not declaring His words then it's hard for Him to move on our faithlessness. As pointed out in Hebrews 11:6, "without faith it is impossible to please God".

When your desires seem to be louder than God's promises, remember that He made promises because He wanted to execute them. Remind yourself that "he satisfies the longing soul, and the hungry soul he fills with good things" (Psalm 107:9).

So if you're hungry for more – you're the perfect candidate for God.

That's also why He created prayer and granted us access to come before His throne boldly. This is a privilege that even angels do not have without meeting certain protocols.

JOURNAL PROMPT

Journal the specific needs or wants on your heart today. Ask God for insight into what current provision He has already sent you to satisfy that need – or what tools are already in your hand to start working towards it.

I AM PROVIDED FOR

> "THE LORD IS THE STRONGHOLD OF MY LIFE, OF WHOM SHALL I BE AFRAID?"
>
> –Psalm 27:1b

PROVISION DAY 2 | I AM PROVIDED FOR

"The Lord is the stronghold of my life, of whom shall I be afraid?"

–Psalm 27:1b

Is your paycheck the stronghold of your life, or the Lord All Mighty?

If He is truly our foundation, why are we more concerned about disappointing our bosses than disobeying God?

Our bosses, family, or friends cannot save us from future events which they are clueless about. God knows everything what is against you or what can potentially harm you – and He is the one who promises to keep you. Thankfully, He is the only one that can, so He is the only one that matters.

Why then do we idolize job security so much? That company is not your provider – God is. Sometimes He chooses to use a business to employ you, and other times He commands a person to give to you. No matter the route, He has to prepare for your needs because He's a Good Father, not a bastard dad.

"And my God will supply every need of yours according to his riches in glory in Christ Jesus." –Philippians 4:19

We cannot please God and continue in fear. Fear will only starve the faith that is necessary to receive His love and clear instruction for your provision. Fortunately for us, His perfect love is committed to casting out all fear (1 John 4:18). So allow His love to guard the provision of peace He has already guaranteed and sent for you.

He's already taken care of your worst enemies (death, hell, & the devil) – so give Him space and permission to handle your "lightweight" troubles also.

JOURNAL PROMPT

Identify all the ways the fear of lack is keeping you from pursuing God wholeheartedly, or from completing a task He put on your heart. Make a commitment to only look to Him as the source of your provision. Confess and meditate on this: God is the unfailing, unlimited source of my supply.

I AM A GOOD INVESTMENT FOR GOD

"FOR THE SONS OF THIS WORLD ARE MORE SHREWD IN DEALING WITH THEIR OWN GENERATION THAN THE SONS OF LIGHT."

–Luke 16:8

PROVISION DAY 3 | I AM A GOOD INVESTMENT FOR GOD

"For the sons of this world are more shrewd in dealing with their own generation than the sons of light."

–Luke 16:8

It is a wise and right thing to establish a return on our talents, especially when done in excellence and for the glory of God. For this reason, it is not holy to squander the resources and gifts God provides without taking responsibility for their value and worth.

Sometimes as believers, it's hard to see the kingdom value in our gifts, especially if you are an entrepreneur or called into ministry. From media and medicine to law and beauty, the Lord desires lordship in all industries - not just in our churches or religious After all he created those industries as well.

It's time to reclaim every business and marketplace genre for the sake of the Good News.

The world spends countless of hours and thousands of dollars in nurturing and perfecting their skills. How much more could we reclaim our generation when we become good stewards over our gifts; reminding the world of how good God is. In doing so, we make a sustainable and eternal impact by creating jobs so others can serve Him.

Ask the Lord to help you be diligent in providing services and products that can scale and grow to serve more and more people. Start small if you need to, but stop belittling or burying the talent given to you by "hobbying" it off for free.

A good steward can show an increase return with time – being stagnant is not godly. (See the story of the talents in Matthew 25:14-30 where Jesus addresses this.)

JOURNAL PROMPT

God's investment in you has value. Establish a price on at least one of your gifts/ services and publish it somewhere. Set a number that works for you, but start setting up a way for people to invest into what you offer, so it can be multiplied and improved with time.

I AM IN GOD'S HOUSE

"AND HE SAID TO HIM, 'SON, YOU ARE ALWAYS WITH ME, AND ALL THAT IS MINE IS YOURS.'"

–Luke 15:31

PROVISION DAY 4 | I AM IN GOD'S HOUSE

"And he said to him, 'Son, you are always with me, and all that is mine is yours.'"

–Luke 15:31

If you're going to be in Christ, don't be found drooling for what's outside. If you've decided to be in the house of God, go to the table & feast! If you're thirsty, drink till you're full. Confused? Request supernatural wisdom on what to do & how to move forward. Bank account looking insufficient? Pray for uncommon favor to complete the daring visions & dreams your heart is dying to see come true.

And please, be specific with your requests.

God can handle your lightweight but stop praying for things you already know how to accomplish. Bring him the heavyweight desires for those good works He prepared you to walk in. ***Stop burying the big ideas, you're here to solve big problems in your generation Esther.*** There is no need for false humility.

The Spirit of the Lord is in you to do great things, and He is not bored. You've actually been saved for a specific part of His kingdom agenda so dig in & find out what it is. You're in His house for such a time as this & all that He has is yours. Be about your Father's very important business and bank on His provision being made available as you make each step in obedience.

"The Lord is my shepherd, I shall not want." – Psalm 23:1

JOURNAL PROMPT

What do you consider to be a "hard request?" Something that you know the provision can't be arrived at by your own means? It's time to acknowledge and write it down in your journal. You lose nothing by looking to God for it to be given supernaturally, but writing it down is the first step of faith and believing that it already exists in God's kingdom. All that's missing is time for it to be manifested – watch and start expecting today.

I CAN ASK FOR WHATEVER I NEED

"IF ANY OF YOU LACKS WISDOM, LET HIM ASK GOD, WHO GIVES GENEROUSLY TO ALL WITHOUT REPROACH, AND IT WILL BE GIVEN HIM."

–James 1:5

PROVISION DAY 5 | I CAN ASK FOR WHATEVER I NEED

"If any of you lacks wisdom, let him ask God, who gives generously to all without reproach, and it will be given him."

–James 1:5

You don't need to have it all when you know the One who does. Let God worry about how your life (or day, or project) will pan out. You just focus on being obedient so you can keep up with Him when He moves.

There is nothing more painful than seeing God open doors supernaturally, but not being able to maximize the opportunity because you weren't ready. #BeenThereDoneThat

Don't get so caught up in the details that aren't perfect, that you miss the progress and how God is granting you favor despite your flawed nature. Missing God's perspective can happen mentally or spiritually, if you allow yourself to get discouraged by the circumstance rather than what God promises to do. There will be many times where you are clueless on what to do in a situation. But this is where it's important to remind yourself that the system is working as designed. You are not God, therefore you were not designed to know everything (Aha!).

But with this Scripture in James embedded in your heart, such limitations become a joyful invitation to draw to God in conversation, rather than be deterred from purpose. Don't let your lack of knowledge invite the lie of hopelessness today. Again, ain't nobody got time for that! :-D

This is all part of the plan to draw you into prayer. "Let us then approach God's throne of grace with confidence, so that we may receive mercy and find grace to help us in our time of need." (Hebrews 4:16)

JOURNAL PROMPT

Invite the Lord to lead every aspect of your routine today. Consult Him in every decision and ASK for what you need to succeed. Be sure to track any prayers that got answered and any concerns that were resolved.

PURITY

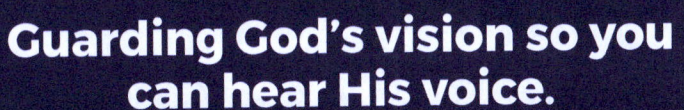

I AM PART OF A FAMILY

"WHOEVER ISOLATES HIMSELF SEEKS HIS OWN DESIRE;
HE BREAKS OUT AGAINST ALL SOUND JUDGMENT."

–Proverbs 18:1

PURITY DAY 1 | I AM PART OF A FAMILY

**"Whoever isolates himself seeks his own desire;
he breaks out against all sound judgment."**

–Proverbs 18:1

Believe it or not, God doesn't see our "go it alone" attitude as smart, he calls it prideful stupidity.

Past hurts and our independent culture will tell us otherwise, but we are not smarter than God. He made the human spirit to thrive in the midst of others with a similar vision, so we must pursue community at all costs. Yes, flawed humans are everywhere – even in the body of Christ. But He did not call us to run alone, so he WILL link us with others who can run alongside us and offer support.

As this African proverb reminds us: "To go fast, go alone. To go far, go together."

We must ask God to heal existing hurts or trust issues we may have, and remember that we are also going to fail others in any relationship. So just be thankful for opportunities to practice mercy towards others when they let you down, and to receive it in return. However, holding on to past offenses as the reason why you must keep to yourself is an ancient bait and tactic from the enemy Himself. Don't be fooled.

You're better off surrounded by an imperfect church any day, than left alone with the devil.

We will surely have low points in the pursuit of purity and understanding God's pleasures, "but woe to him who is alone when he falls and has not another to lift him up!" (Ecclesiastes 4:10)

JOURNAL PROMPT

Make community your priority today if you've been feeling lonely or isolated. But it doesn't matter if you feel okay being alone right now. Ask the Lord to lead you to a small group, church, or group of believers with the same vision, so you can stay edified and endure this race for the long haul.

I LIVE IN THE LIGHT

"THEREFORE, I WILL BOAST ALL THE MORE GLADLY OF MY WEAKNESSES, SO THAT THE POWER OF CHRIST MAY REST UPON ME."

–2 Corinthians 12:9

PURITY DAY 2 | I LIVE IN THE LIGHT

"Therefore, I will boast all the more gladly of my weaknesses, so that the power of Christ may rest upon me."

–2 Corinthians 12:9

Let's be honest. No one likes to brag about their flaws. Yet, Paul is pretty much encouraging us in this verse to snitch on our flesh regularly.

Yes, we are weak physically but, we have a mighty God who made us that way so He could showcase His power through us. Plus, Paul knows that the enemy's temptations only have power in darkness, so boasting in our struggles and putting them in the light takes the fight to the enemy before he has a chance to get comfortable and overpower us with guilt.

Moreover, sinful thoughts or hidden habits don't have time to get a grip on us when we give godly friends the permission to till the soil of our heart frequently. So it's worth the energy to share life with others, and boast in your failures. Shame is just the accuser's attempt at pulling you outside of the finished work of Christ.

So confessing to an accountability partner or sharing your testimony in public is the best way to remind Him that the price has already been paid – IN FULL. There's no need for you to pay again by retreating and wallowing in guilt.

Acknowledge the godly sorrow, but share your story unashamed. This is more for you than it is for "them" anyway.

Forget flawless, you're forgiven.

JOURNAL PROMPT

Find 2-3 today people who you can give "full refrigerator rights" to. Let them know they have an all access pass to ask the hard questions or call out your shady activities in love. It will frustrate your enemy like nothing else can.

I HAVE AUTHORITY

"So Christ, having been offered once to bear the sins of many, will appear a second time, not to deal with sin but to save those who are eagerly waiting for him."

–Hebrews 9:28

PURITY DAY 3 | I HAVE AUTHORITY

"So Christ, having been offered once to bear the sins of many, will appear a second time, not to deal with sin but to save those who are eagerly waiting for him."

–Hebrews 9:28

We can't keeping making excuses for our sin, when Christ already died for that.

It's pointless waiting for a big breakthrough to free you from your vices, when God's made it clear the only reason He'll be showing up again is to scoop up His saints. But until then, it's up to us to respond to His victory over the enemy and repent (read: remind sin that it's no longer your boss) and

We do this by using Jesus' revealed Word to continuously declare our position of authority over darkness, submit wayward thoughts to Christ and vocally resist temptation. James 4:7

promises that this strategy works for having the devil flee, along with his seductions.

And when I say vocally resist temptation, I mean stating out loud that "XYZ" sin has no dominion on you, since you are now dominated by the Holy Spirit. Since my software consulting job required that I travel every week and live in hotel rooms by myself – I would literally be shouting out verses in my suite against lustful thoughts. Too many times we try to convince ourselves in our head that we're strong enough – which usually fails because that's not the strategy God gave us.

He didn't ask us to convince ourselves that we're strong enough – He said resist. When is the last time you tried to resist someone with your mind? How did that work out? You resist by audibly and authoritatively letting the person and everyone in the vicinity know that you do not agree and will be taking no part in their activities. Right?!

Beloved, purity is a Person whom has already overcome for us, so purity is possible. Don't wait for a deliverer or sign. He already came and his name is Christ.

JOURNAL PROMPT

What fear or pleasure itch is this recurring sin temporarily satisfying in your life? Exposing the root desire that is causing you to return to your vomit will help you turn the specific desire over to Christ instead. What pleasure or promise has God provided for this desire that you're really craving? God is not intimidated by your sex drive or need for pleasure – He created you that way so He has an answer for it. If you're not sure – pray and ask.

I SEE WHAT GOD SEES

―――――

"BLESSED ARE THE PURE IN HEART, FOR THEY SHALL SEE GOD."

–Matthew 5:8

―――――

PURITY DAY 4 | I SEE WHAT GOD SEES

"Blessed are the pure in heart, for they shall see God."

–Matthew 5:8

You were created because God had a desire for you. Nothing else matters when framed with that truth. No distractions or circumstances add up to a valid excuse in light of this one responsibility - to know God and be known by Him. Meditate on this today and let all other desires fall back into submission where they belong - second to knowing Christ and Him crucified for you.

It's so much bigger than just "not having sex". It's about knowing and abiding in His words. Purity just flows from the fresh perspective and passions God gives you as a result. He doesn't care about the external pretending, but transforming the desires of your heart. Holy Spirit now does the work so you can gain victory and move on to the next one. Because, yes, there is other territory to claim.

God made you for friendship with Him. Don't be deceived now by the sway of this world to let God's gifts consume your time and loyalty to Him. The earth is the Lord's and everything in it, so He will move mountains for the righteous ones who know His will because they seek His face. Be still, and know that He is God. Make room for Him only, and He'll make room for everything else in your life.

"Therefore, if anyone cleanses himself from what is dishonorable, he will be a vessel for honorable use, set apart as holy, useful to the master of the house, ready for every good work." -2 Timothy 2:21

JOURNAL PROMPT

Meditate on 1 Corinthians 2:9-10 and ask God to show you anything in your life distorting your vision of those things prepared for you. Then Ask forgiveness in prayer and turn from those habits or people as they come to mind. Welcome the Holy Spirit so He can now show you what He speaks of in verse Matthew 5:10.

I AM GOD'S RESTING PLACE

"DO YOU NOT KNOW THAT YOUR BODIES ARE TEMPLES OF THE HOLY SPIRIT, WHO IS IN YOU, WHOM YOU HAVE RECEIVED FROM GOD?"

–1 Corinthians 6:19

PURITY DAY 5 | I AM GOD'S RESTING PLACE

"Do you not know that your bodies are temples of the Holy Spirit, who is in you, whom you have received from God?"

–1 Corinthians 6:19

Yes, guarding your time, eyes and ears from foolishness so that you are ready to receive and relay the things of God is not a passing hobby. It will take diligence and discipline. We just have to be honest with ourselves and remember that not all things are beneficial, even if permissible (1 Corinthians 6:12).

But the gains outweigh the losses here. Most people think purity equals giving up fun to gain boredom, so of course they skip the transaction.

Yet, purity is only as boring as you make it.

If you find yourself free to enjoy God and release righteousness on the earth, yet decide to sit on Facebook all day, that's your idea of adventure - not God's.

Jesus did not save you to tame you. And He only operates from passionate purpose and pleasure. So if He is living on the inside of you, He's hoping to use your unique personality and skills to carry out this amazing kingdom adventure.

We're often waiting for some booming audible voice, but the answer is already clear and the way He's wired you. Your design is custom-fitted to the way God wants to reach people through you, in a way that only you can. Review the questions in the back of this devotional for some ideas.

JOURNAL PROMPT

*Turn to the **Pinpointing Purpose section** at the very end of this book, and answer the 12 questions provided. Review them and look for common themes and patterns to identify the kind of purpose party God wants to get going in you and through you. Journal what you believe these things say about your purpose, and how God wants to manifest Himself through you.*

COURAGE

Being confident about your Father's business.

I AM LOVED

> "O MAN GREATLY LOVED, FEAR NOT, PEACE BE WITH YOU; BE STRONG AND OF GOOD COURAGE."

–Daniel 10:19a

COURAGE DAY 1 | I AM LOVED

"O man greatly loved, fear not, peace be with you; be strong and of good courage."

–Daniel 10:19a

One of the most courageous things a woman can do is embrace the reality that she is uniquely and unconditionally loved, forever. Yet, it's true – and one of the first steps to living and finishing fearlessly. Beloved, it's time to stop asking fear for permission to do the things faith has already released you to.

Fear is only the knockoff brand of faith. They both ask you to imagine things that don't yet exist, see it as real, and live out your life accordingly.

However, God is the original designer of this faith lifestyle and backs it up with His very own power and presence. He alone can guarantee true success, security, and satisfaction. Fear only came about after as the counterfeit to distract you from God's original design and awesome agenda.

Fear tells you faith is too costly and claims to offer a cheaper alternative that allows you to remain in your comfort zone. But as we know, the comfort zone produces nothing new and suffocates dreams before they even get a chance to wake up.

If feeling overwhelmed by fear, remember that both faith and fear are largely the result of habits. So decide which one you will feed going forward.

Indulge in the Word and love of God this week, and it will start to expose fear for the liar it really is. "There is no fear in love, but perfect love casts out fear. For fear has to do with punishment, and whoever fears has not been perfected in love." (1 John 4:18).

God is with you, what can man do to you?

JOURNAL PROMPT

The best diet for faith to thrive is the pure and unfiltered Word of God. Spend some time reading through an entire book of the Bible in one sitting. If it sounds intimidating, start small with a book such as Philippians or Colossians which only has 4 chapters. Even if you feel nothing happening, your spirit man is feasting, trust me. Do this regularly and you'll be able to witness the effects soon after.

I AM ALLERGIC TO ANXIETY

"DO NOT BE ANXIOUS ABOUT ANYTHING, BUT IN EVERYTHING BY PRAYER AND SUPPLICATION WITH THANKSGIVING, LET YOUR REQUESTS BE MADE KNOWN TO GOD."

–Philippians 4:6

COURAGE DAY 2 | I AM ALLERGIC TO ANXIETY

"Do not be anxious about anything, but in everything by prayer and supplication with thanksgiving, let your requests be made known to God."

–Philippians 4:6

If God is not the answer, you're asking the wrong question. God has promised to never withhold any good thing from you. Which means, if you do not have something in your life right now, it must not be good for this season (Psalm 84:11). Maybe you're forcing something that's outside of the will of God, or wanting it before the appointed time. Either way, it's not worth the stress trying to live life outside of God's help.

So identify any worries that you are currently allowing to bog you down in anxiety. Unchecked desires will only lead to doubting God's power and love for you, so be bold in bringing them before God promptly. All of them.

If there are valid issues overwhelming you, ask God for wisdom on how to handle them (James 1:5). Trying to figure out solutions on your own is a dangerous game of playing God, and will eventually produce pride and resentment. So let's return to the source, and allow Him to be the God that He is. His power is made perfect in your weakness anyway.

Therefore, focus on getting so wrapped up in God's glory that you become allergic to any words or feelings of anxiety that would downplay His power. Get so obsessed with His promises that you can tell all mental objections to "Shut up!"

Get addicted to your purpose, so you can develop an adverse reaction to your excuses. And when you encounter a limitation – celebrate the miracle of how God's going to use you anyway. Because as we know, He qualifies the called, He doesn't call the qualified.

"Therefore I will boast all the more gladly of my weaknesses, so that the power of Christ may rest upon me" (2 Corinthians 12:9).

JOURNAL PROMPT

God commands us not to be anxious for anything (Philippians 4:6). So confess ALL of your doubts and anxieties to God today – and repent (read: change your mind and choose to no longer agree with them). When anxiety tries to attack you, ask Him for the grace to see His power and sovereignty over the circumstance instead.

I FIGHT FOR MY INHERITANCE

"FROM THE DAYS OF JOHN THE BAPTIST UNTIL NOW THE KINGDOM OF HEAVEN HAS SUFFERED VIOLENCE, AND THE VIOLENT TAKE IT BY FORCE."

–Matthew 11:12

COURAGE DAY 3 | I FIGHT FOR MY INHERITANCE

"From the days of John the Baptist until now the kingdom of heaven has suffered violence, and the violent take it by force."

–Matthew 11:12

One cannot go timidly into the promises of God. We must run, press and war to get in. For the Kingdom advances boldly, and only the bold will pursue it relentlessly. Only those confident in their spiritual inheritance will cling to it until it produces fruit in their natural and personal lives.

"The wicked flee when no one pursues, but the righteous are bold as a lion." –Proverbs 28:1

But such confidence only comes from knowing the Word and what it says about your Kingdom identity and life. Otherwise, you won't even know you're leaving money on the table.

And you can't afford to leave promises un-hatched. That's the very reason Christ died. It's the very reason you surrendered your life to Him for greater.

If not, what else did you come to Jesus looking for? Why else believe in a great God? How else will you find the motivation and endurance needed to finish strong? We can't keep prioritizing our earthly routines yet expecting the heavenly results and freedom we really crave.

Eternity has been imprinted into your heart, so you will never be satisfied with this world's provision. Ask God for what His Word says is yours. His promise was on earth, heaven – but it has to start with you.

JOURNAL PROMPT

Write down 3 things promised to you in the Bible (i.e. peace from John 14:27). Now write out a decision to always use your right pursue and defend these realities, no matter the circumstance you find yourself in going forward.

I AM THE LIGHT IN THE ROOM

"IN THE SAME WAY, LET YOUR LIGHT SHINE BEFORE OTHERS, SO THEY MAY SEE YOUR GOOD WORKS AND GIVE GLORY TO YOUR FATHER WHO IS IN HEAVEN."

–Matthew 5:16

COURAGE DAY 4 | I AM THE LIGHT IN THE ROOM

"In the same way, let your light shine before others, so they may see your good works and give glory to your Father who is in heaven."

–Matthew 5:16

Your talent and skills have been given to you for such a time as this. Even more, you have been placed in the city and surroundings you're in for such a time as this.

The Holy Spirit did not light your heart with life for you to live under a bubble beloved. Yes, Christianity is personal but it's definitely not private. Come out of the closet and go public with His good news!

Even more, all your gifts have been freely given to you to aide in the telling of this exciting message. Set your talents on fire with the passion of Christ, then get up on a platform so they can give light to all in the house. Whether its medicine, modeling, or managing paper clip shipments – the excellence of your work should draw the attention of those in your industry. Your creative solutions and people ethics should challenge your peers to do business better and to improve whatever community they're in.

You have the resurrection living on the inside of you – you have the answer. Let's sharpen our skills and serve our cultures so well, they can't help but see our works and glorify our great God!

Because a woman of God should always be confident of the vision and value she brings to every room.

JOURNAL PROMPT

Spend some time perfecting your craft this week. Set aside some time to sharpen the gifts God has given you for the Kingdom.

I SERVE CHRIST ONLY

"IF I WERE STILL TRYING TO PLEASE MAN, I WOULD NOT BE A SERVANT OF CHRIST."

–Galatians 1:10b

COURAGE DAY 5 | I SERVE CHRIST ONLY

"If I were still trying to please man, I would not be a servant of Christ."

–Galatians 1:10b

Live like you're dying, because you are. Let this sober truth remind you of how much you have to lose in following God: NOTHING.

You will be losing it all in death anyway, so focus on what's really eternal. People and possessions cannot keep you from the only thing worse than physical death – dying spiritually. So let's prioritize what's important and stop making excuses for the people we allow to influence us.

Ask God what His plans are for you today, and decide to obey. He alone can bring you relationships or accomplishments that go beyond what you can hold on to personally. God's plans and instructions weave you into the bigger picture that will endure even after you're gone.

Sooner or later you'll realize that only you can give an account for what you did with your life. So pick sooner. Let's filter everyone else's words through God's enduring Word today.

Because only what is done for Christ will last. And only what is done with Christ can.

I have the right to do anything--but I will not be mastered by anything. -1 Corinthians 6:12

JOURNAL PROMPT

Decide once and for all to pursue your purpose because God said so. Write out this declaration and final stance, and list any competing idols in your life that you now submit to Christ's will alone. Now thank God that you only have one master to please. All others can bow.all.the.way.down.

FOCUS

Making heaven's purpose your priority.

I PURSUE PURPOSE NOT PAPER

"LEAVE THE DEAD TO BURY THE DEAD. BUT AS FOR YOU, GO AND PROCLAIM THE KINGDOM OF GOD."

–Luke 9:60

FOCUS DAY 1 | I PURSUE PURPOSE NOT PAPER

"Leave the dead to bury the dead. But as for you, go and proclaim the kingdom of God."

–Luke 9:60

Let's put Jesus' words in a more current light. "Let your coworker rack up every certification known to man because corporate America can lay you off at any moment. But as for you, focus on excelling in exactly what I've called you to."

Of course, acquiring certifications are not sinful and are actually good to develop yourself in your committed field. But if motivated by fear or the worried culture around you, it becomes disobedience and a distraction to why God has positioned you where you are. You know that **pursuing purpose will bring the paper, not the other way around.**

Unlike those working for themselves, you know you are under the main contract of "advancing heaven into earth". So doors that God opens for you in a job, neighborhood, or creative team are opportunities to bring His light and prosperous worldview to that sphere of influence. Your main job description is to re-present Christ and His heart to those around you. What a privilege!

May your heavenly agenda be the fuel and strength you need to carry out this week's tasks with joy and focus.

Remember why you started.

JOURNAL PROMPT

What's one thing you can do today to move you forward in your purpose? Remind yourself of what excited you in the beginning, and create a clear list of steps towards that end goal. Breaking down the vision will help you prepare for the journey, instead of trying to sprint.

I DOMINATE MY DESIRES

"TURN MY EYES AWAY FROM WORTHLESS THINGS;
PRESERVE MY LIFE ACCORDING TO YOUR WORD."

–Psalm 119:37

FOCUS DAY 2 | I DOMINATE MY DESIRES

**"Turn my eyes away from worthless things;
preserve my life according to your word."**

–Psalm 119:37

Your goals don't care how you feel and neither should you. It's time to stop babying your flesh. It is okay to tell your emotions "NO" at times to establish who's in control. As Romans 8:14 reminds us, your spirit man leads and sets the rules. Not the other way around, because your feelings are like that toddler who throws a tantrum every 2 hours. At some point, you just have to zone them out so they eventually learn who is in control.

Yes, you have to live in the real world, but if there are any distractions that can be cut, it's time for them to go! And don't be apologetic about it either. Sometimes we're more concerned about missing out on earthly things than missing out on heaven-on-earth.

Even if something is not direct sin, it's often good to fast physical pleasures to be more in tune with your spiritual taste buds. It's like saying no to your coworker's junk food so you can preserve your appetite for mama's three course meal at home.

"All things are lawful," but not all things are helpful. "All things are lawful," but not all things build up (1 Corinthians 10:23). Perspective is everything. Therefore, you must frequently review the benefits that come with pursuing purpose. That way, you can quickly identify worthless relationships and habits that you pick up with time.

Again, remind yourself that you can't afford to keep settling for good at the expense of great.

JOURNAL PROMPT

Write down a list of your closest friends (3-5). Do any of them know your goals, or share the same vision to complete God's call on their life? If not, pray and ask God to give you favor with a new community of women, and a mentor that will draw His best out of you.

I FEED MY SPIRIT MAN

> "'Man shall not live by bread alone, but by every word that comes from the mouth of God.'"

–Matthew 4:4

FOCUS DAY 3 | I FEED MY SPIRIT MAN

"'Man shall not live by bread alone, but by every word that comes from the mouth of God.'"

–Matthew 4:4

Instead of falling into hopelessness when you fall short and lose strength to focus, see it as your spirit man signaling you to eat! If you can no longer see the point for pursuing your passions, take stock to see when you last feasted on the Word of God.

Those Instagram quotes can only take you so far. We should taste and see that the Lord is good, but then continue chewing on the Word until we are full! If not, you neglect your spiritual appetite and eventually turn to your shallow emotional cravings in an attempt to scratch the itch.

Yet, unlike those in the world who sample random palettes trying to find what they're searching for – we know what our body needs. Don't envy the walking dead because they seem content on the world's junk food. Their frequent sugar highs also end in frequent empty lows. I mean, just listen to their roller coaster love songs. Constantly indulging in the next quick fix only ends in spiritual malnutrition and starvation.

Return to the Lord and eat and drink freely from His Word and Spirit, where the bread and living water run freely with no cost to your soul (John 7:37). Plus, constant Bible-reading reminds you that: **You don't need to know it all when you know the One who does.**

JOURNAL PROMPT

Like any healthy appetite, you must make the decision to eat for nutrition and not for taste. Do you run to the Word before you're starving, or is it an acquired taste (that you still haven't acquired?) Start cultivating a spiritual diet today by reading all of Isaiah 55 in one sitting – yummy! Verse 11 is my favorite.

I PLAY TO WIN

"THEREFORE DO NOT BE FOOLISH, BUT UNDERSTAND WHAT THE WILL OF THE LORD IS."

–Ephesians 5:17

FOCUS DAY 4 | I PLAY TO WIN

"Therefore do not be foolish, but understand what the will of the Lord is."

–Ephesians 5:17

Lionheart, I keep drilling this point but you must decide once and for all which team you're going to play for. That is the only way to establish which coach to listen to, and to know where you are going to end up.

So many times, we're lusting too much after what the world is doing to even notice God's moves on the field. When not on the bench, we wander into the game with lack of purpose and find ourselves asking *"How far can I compromise without sinning?"* rather than *"How far can I go with God?"*

If you still find yourself asking the former question frequently, you are most likely scoring points for the wrong team! Asking "How far is too far before its sin" will only produce a life where you keep getting pushed into the sin end zone. If godly sorrow is flooding your heart because you realize how much this wastes God's goodness, just pray and ask right now for His help to refocus.

Jesus didn't save you on layaway.

Your eternity and success has already been fully paid for. So play to win.

JOURNAL PROMPT

Ask God to remind you of the high price that was paid for your freedom and to turn your focus back to Him. Recommit to playing for heaven's team if you're going to wear the jersey of being "Christian". Journal a prayer of commitment or recommitment to your passions if necessary.

I MOVE WITH CLARITY & STRATEGY

"LOOK CAREFULLY THEN HOW YOU WALK, NOT AS UNWISE BUT AS WISE, MAKING THE BEST USE OF THE TIME, BECAUSE THE DAYS ARE EVIL."

—Ephesians 5:15-16

FOCUS DAY 5 | I MOVE WITH CLARITY & STRATEGY

"Look carefully then how you walk, not as unwise but as wise, making the best use of the time, because the days are evil."

—Ephesians 5:15-16

Now that you've repented for aimlessly wandering around on the field at times, let's get an understanding for the privileged position you've been called to on God's team. Like your Father, you operate from wisdom - knowing what to do in each situation. So you must refuse to settle in confusion.

However, this wisdom comes from knowing His word for yourself. Waiting 'til Sunday to hear the pastor preach will leave you clueless on what to do Monday through Saturday when you're alone.

Your time also becomes more valuable because you realize it's only been given to you for a season – to accomplish specific tasks.

Another year will quickly pass, but instead of just waiting for Beyoncé or Drake to drop their next album, you will better know the Lord and understand your purpose: aka your goal and touchdown.

There is now a joy in knowing where you're headed and how to play to win.

You know what you're saved for, so you don't wander back to what you were saved from.

JOURNAL PROMPT

Spend some time in prayer to pinpoint why God has you at the job, church, or house where He's currently placed you. Meditate on how you felt when you first got the job or the relationships you've made. How can you improve those circles you're in? Remembering your passion and reason for being where you are now will bring much more focus and productivity to your tasks.

PASSION

Pursuing God's call without apology.

I AM FREE, PERIOD.

"IT IS FOR FREEDOM CHRIST HAS SET US FREE, STAND FIRM THEREFORE, AND DO NOT SUBMIT AGAIN TO A YOKE OF SLAVERY."

–Galatians 5:1

PASSION DAY 1 | I AM FREE, PERIOD.

"It is for freedom Christ has set us free, stand firm therefore, and do not submit again to a yoke of slavery."

–Galatians 5:1

Lionheart, before we can dive into your passions, this truth in Galatians 5:1 has to become your reality. It is for freedom you've been unchained from your sin – not for boredom, fear, or confusion. So why continue to live in those cages?

You were saved on purpose, for a purpose.

Believe the good report of the Lord and advance into the gifts, talents, and peace He has promised will "make room" for you (Proverbs 18:16).

Quit longing for Egypt and the fleeting delicacies of sin. No matter how "good" the memories from your old life now seem, remember that you were a slave with no hope of knowing God intimately.

God is greater than the sin He rescued you from.

And He called you out by name so you could taste and see for yourself! He didn't call you out of false happiness to give you nothing – He wants you to know true pleasure. Even more, God wants to give you enjoyable gifts so you can be an oasis in the earth. That way, others can pass through your life and experience His abundant kindness commitment to "living lit". (John 10:10)

You're free to obsess over passions that feel good for eternity beloved. Boredom, fear, and confusion no longer have authority to bind you with their opinions, so feel free to look them in the eye today and say #ByeFelicia!

JOURNAL PROMPT

Take a picture of Galatians 5:1 on your phone and set it as your screensaver. Meditate on it throughout the day and try to say it from memory. Then declare it out loud whenever fear or confusion tell you that you have no purpose. Passion begins with this essential ingredient - freedom!

I AM WIRED TO WIN

"JESUS SAID TO THEM, 'MY FOOD IS TO DO THE WILL OF HIM WHO SENT ME AND TO ACCOMPLISH HIS WORK.'"

–John 4:34

PASSION DAY 2 | I AM WIRED TO WIN

"Jesus said to them, 'My food is to do the will of him who sent me and to accomplish his work.'"

–John 4:34

Why did God design you the way He did, and wire you with your peculiar personality?

Without knowing this, everything you do will be a shot in the dark and a mere hoping for happily ever after. But when you realize that you have been specifically fashioned for success in a specific gifting and path, living becomes an easy yolk.

Your unique identity becomes a treasure that you guard with your life instead of pawning it for another "popular" option. And the spirit of the Lord becomes the very necessary fuel for solving that problem that you were sent here to resolve.

Jesus took the time to pinpoint His purpose before He jumped into ministry and fame, so it kept Him from getting weary or sidetracked when circumstances got hectic. In the same way, you must slow down and ask God to give you the direction for each season you find yourself. Find out who you are and why all your parts add up to a whole in God's eyes - because He makes all things well.

There's nothing like knowing God's heart for you and those around you.

Only then do you get excited about seeing it come to pass with each step of obedience. It brings a satisfaction and passion like no other!

JOURNAL PROMPT

Imagine you just got sentenced to prison for the next 50 years. What are 3 things you're sad about not experiencing or completing? Now write them down and be thankful for what you have and where you are right now. Make your freedom count today!

I AM CHOSEN

> "YOU DID NOT CHOOSE ME, BUT I CHOSE YOU AND APPOINTED YOU THAT YOU SHOULD GO AND BEAR FRUIT..."

–John 15:16a

PASSION DAY 3 | I AM CHOSEN

"You did not choose me, but I chose you and appointed you that you should go and bear fruit..."

–John 15:16a

Fitting in is not an option. You were chosen for this. As a daughter of the King, you have been called out for purpose. The Holy Spirit has now been given to you, so that you can stand out. Why smother such a royal mark to become relevant, when that's the best part about your new identity?

The Holy Spirit allows you to bring results to your culture and circle, which will in turn make you relevant to their needs. Not the other way around. Yet, we get so deceived into pursuing society's way of living, hoping we can then draw their attention to how relatable and good God is. But that's so unnecessary.

God is relatable and good, all by Himself.

Remember where your true influence and success comes from - from the Lord. And believe it or not, the world is actually watching to see if we as Christians will bring something different to the table to tackle today's many current issues. So it is foolish to cheat them, and yourself, by trying to hide the very thing that they need to see at work – the power of God at work in you.

Never apologize for pursuing the passions God burdens you with.

Even if you are not fully clear on what your specific gifts are, Isaiah 61:1 lets you in on your main purpose, no matter what season we're in. Your generation is desperately seeking supernatural answers and unshakeable love. It's time to plug into the Holy Spirit and shine!

JOURNAL PROMPT

Read Isaiah 61:1 then thank God for the gift of the Holy Spirit. Ask Him to fill you even more, so that you can carry out your main call and heaven's passion to preach the good news and declare freedom to those around you.

I RUN WITH THE VISION

"WHERE THERE IS NO PROPHETIC VISION THE PEOPLE CAST OFF RESTRAINT."

-Proverbs 29:18

PASSION DAY 4 | I RUN WITH THE VISION

"Where there is no prophetic vision the people cast off restraint."

-Proverbs 29:18

Contrary to popular belief sis, seeing is not believing when you're in relationship with God. Instead, what you believe is what you will eventually see.

So if you can see it coming up in your mind frequently, you need to write it down. Then, as this vision becomes clearer, you'll find yourself restraining from distracting activities to pursue what you now believe is possible.

Put simply, you have to see it before you see it.

Having that vision written down starts helping you prioritize those passions in your schedule. And you'll begin searching for ways to sharpen your gifts so you can move closer to seeing the vision realized.

Purpose driven habits also give healthy direction to your passions, instead of letting them seep out in idle hands. For example, don't just focus on not watching that TV show or not wasting hours on Instagram. Your mind will just keep spinning in guilt and defeat. Plus, those habits will only return if the real issue of discontentment is not dealt with. Switch to the offensive instead and give yourself permission to GO ALL IN with tasks that will actually bring your dreams to life.

Don't just write the vision down, run with it.

Because really, there is no in between: **Be purpose driven, or be wasting time.**

JOURNAL PROMPT

Create a vision board of words or images driving you towards your purpose. If you already have a passion board, how can you refresh it to keep you motivated and excited towards your goals? Keeping your focus in front of you is important to avoid distractions and time-wasting.

I FINISH WHAT I START

"Jesus replied, 'No one who puts a hand to the plow and looks back is fit for service in the Kingdom of God.'"

–Luke 9:62

PASSION DAY 5 | I FINISH WHAT I START

"Jesus replied, 'No one who puts a hand to the plow and looks back is fit for service in the kingdom of God.'"

–Luke 9:62

With all the brokenness and perversion in the Earth, there is so much opportunity for the Holy Spirit to work. And not only is He able to move, but He is willing and waiting to act. However, we are His hands and feet so will we permit Him to finish what He started in and through us? Will we finally kick procrastination and perfectionism off God's throne and confidently complete the call on our lives?

See, the heavens belong to the Lord, but the Earth He has given to the children of man (Psalm 115:16). So for earthly matters, God positions us as salt of the earth, to be channels of His grace. Instead of complaining about all the changes that are needed in society, let's remember that it's why we're still here! so more light can shine in the darkness!

Your words and works are the vessel that allow Him to showcase His power over sin – not just in your life, but for all those in your sphere of influence. That's your awesome privilege and purpose. Every passion you take action on is another chapter forward in seeing kingdom impact in your family and generation.

God's way works, so don't stop putting one foot in front of the other until you see the results He painted on your imagination. Your dreams for your culture and family are valid, but you alone carry the authority

Trust Him and just start by finishing the last thing He asked you to do.

You've been called – answer!

JOURNAL PROMPT

Which overlooked needs in your culture currently frustrate you? Write what you see as possible solutions or things not being done about it. Now take action towards seeing those results and don't quit until you're finished!

JOURNAL PROMPTS

PINPOINTING PURPOSE

Answer all 12 questions, then review for common themes, passions and skills.

1) **What passages in the Bible really get you excited or filled with hope?** Look them up in your Bible or on Google, and write down 3-5 of the ones that really get you fired up.

2) **What do friends and families always ask you to do for them**? Write down whatever comes to mind. (i.e. plan events or fix laptop)

3) **Who are the mentors or role models that you follow or pay attention to?** List them all and write down how have they helped you grow or what about them do you admire.

4) **What do you "waste time" doing when not on the job**? Write down the projects or places that you escape to on your down time.

5) **Which overlooked needs in your culture currently frustrate you?** Write what you see as possible solutions or things not being done about it. Now take action towards seeing those results and don't quit until you're finished!

6) **What issues do you notice in the Christian culture that make you sad?** Write down 2-3 things that concern you or sometimes push you away from churches. How can you act to improve one of these areas since you also represent the church to your peers?

7) **What do you see or imagine when you pray and daydream?** Write down a few of the recurring visions of yourself or society you notice when you let your mind wander.

8) **Is there a common struggle or need you frequently notice when chatting with your friends?** Write down what you wish you could do to help them if you had the time or resources.

9) **What advice do people always ask you for**? Why do you think they see you as knowledgeable in these areas? Write down a one way you can package this information so it can more readily be shared with the next person that asks.

10) **What attracted you to your current church?** Write down which core values attracted you to it and why. (i.e. they value hospitality, encourage creativity, or communicate Biblical messages clearly)

11) **What do you quickly offer to do or help with for free?** Write down 1-2 ways you can monetize these passions to free up yourself to produce more work in these areas.

12) **If you received a billion dollars, what's the first thing you would do to help others?** Write down ways you can start serving in this area using what you can, where you are. Even if you don't have a billion dollars, God has given you something that someone else needs.

WOMEN WHO FINISH

"The master said, '**Well done**, my good and faithful servant. You have been faithful in handling this small amount, so now I will give you many more responsibilities. Let's celebrate together!'

--Matthew 25:23

www.womenwhofinish.com

www.ingramcontent.com/pod-product-compliance
Lightning Source LLC
Chambersburg PA
CBHW071426150426
43191CB00008B/1055